ISLE OF MAN RAILWAYS

Gordon Edgar

AMBERLEY

Front cover image: This could almost be the 10.20 Douglas–Ramsey service near Kirk Michael in the early 1960s, but in reality a special charter train at Keristal during the early evening of 9 April 2013 with No. 8 *Fenella*. The Mediterranean look of the Irish Sea is a phenomenon that the author has also observed along the Cumbrian Coast under certain lighting conditions. Don't be fooled by the idyllic mid-summer look of this photograph; the easterly wind here was unforgiving!

Back cover image: No. 8 *Fenella* has almost reached the summit of the climb from Douglas near Keristal before making the descent down to Port Soderick station on 9 April 2013.

First published 2014

Amberley Publishing
The Hill, Stroud
Gloucestershire, GL5 4EP

www.amberley-books.com

Copyright © Gordon Edgar, 2014

The right of Gordon Edgar to be identified as the Author of this work has been asserted in accordance with the Copyrights, Designs and Patents Act 1988.

ISBN 978 1 4456 3964 2 (print)
ISBN 978 1 4456 3976 5 (ebook)

British Library Cataloguing in Publication Data. A catalogue record for this book is available from the British Library.

Typeset in 9.5pt on 12pt Celeste.
Typesetting by Amberley Publishing.
Printed in the UK.

Introduction

I was very fortunate in having the opportunity to make my first visit to the railways of the Isle of Man in June 1968. At the age of fifteen, and when steam on British Rail (BR) was all but finished, I had a desire to experience a breath of fresh air during those depressing months. The Isle of Man Railway operation had just been leased by Lord Ailsa during the previous year, the fleet of operational locomotives had received a striking new 'Apple Green' livery (now referred to as 'Ailsa Green') and the coastal towns of Port Erin, Peel and Ramsey were still served by the enchanting Victorian steam railway. During the four days that I spent there, based at Douglas which was still very much a traditional holiday destination at that time, I was able to travel on all the lines around the island and right from my first day I was totally captivated by the atmosphere and charm of not just the railways, but also of the island itself. The predominant use of steam traction on the Isle of Man Steam Railway was an incredible step back in time even then, and the delightful Victorian non-corridor coaches, with their leather straps for the droplight windows, immediately took me back to earlier childhood memories of rail travel on the Isle of Wight railways. While work-weary Stanier locomotives were eking out their final existence in the north-west of England at Carnforth, just 70 miles due east of Douglas across the Irish Sea, here was a different world, and the revival of the Isle of Man Steam Railway by Lord Ailsa offered much hope for the future to islanders and tourists alike.

Little was I to know at the time that just over three months after those most memorable railway journeys to St John's, Peel and Ramsey, the lines would be closed for good. With no steam traction working on BR, followed closely by the Isle of Man, the latter part of 1968 was indeed quite a depressing time for the steam railway enthusiast. Fortuitously, with the financial backing of the Isle of Man government, services on the Douglas Port Erin line were subsequently reinstated. For the following ten years fortunes for the steam railway were somewhat mixed, with much rationalisation taking place, including the removal of the fine station canopies at Douglas in 1978, selling off much railway land, the scrapping of surplus rolling stock and the terminal removal of the Ramsey and Peel railway lines.

The Manx Electric (MER) and Snaefell Mountain (SMR) Railways have been more fortunate and their future has never really been threatened, despite the downturn in the island's holiday trade. Although holidaymakers provided the MER with its principal source of income, the line continued to operate year round as it offered a much-needed lifeline for some of the small, isolated communities located along its route.

The Isle of Man Steam Railway of today is a unique microcosm of Victorian railway elegance and is quite unique in the British Isles in possessing the original locomotives, rolling stock and some infrastructure surviving from its original conception in the nineteenth century. In fact, the very early standardisation of locomotives and spare parts has probably been a major factor in the railway's survival right up to the present day. The fifteen standard 2-4-0 tank locomotives supplied to the Isle of Man Railway Co. Ltd were built by Messrs Beyer Peacock of Gorton works, Manchester, over a fifty-three-year period, starting with the first batch of three engines being delivered in time for the opening of the Peel line in 1873. They were all built to the same basic design, but with each subsequent batch being of a larger capacity to counter the increasing traffic demands placed on the railway each year as the island grew in popularity as the 'playground of the North West'. This design was not totally unique to the Isle of Man; the origins of these engines can in fact be found in earlier locomotive designs from the same maker such as those supplied to the Norwegian State Railways in 1871. The elegant Manx Beyer Peacock 2-4-0 tank locomotives are well known by rail enthusiasts around the world and symbolise the Isle of Man, even if at first glance they all look identical. However, a closer study will soon reveal that they are all in fact very different, as identified in some of the photographs in this book.

There have been numerous technical and historical publications and magazine articles covering the railways of the Isle of Man, and quite understandably so. The purpose of this book is to cover pictorially the 1950/1960s period, interspersed with contemporary images, which hopefully will go some way to conveying that magical charm of the island's railways that I first encountered over forty-five years ago, and which can thankfully still be experienced today. Some of the photographs are arranged in a form of a journey around the island commencing at Douglas, and others just convey a particular common theme. Photographs were taken by the author unless otherwise stated.

The island's remaining railways celebrate 140 years of operation, moving into the future with purposefulness and confidence. Long may this living monument to Victorian travel continue to prosper.

I am indebted to Ian Quiggin for meticulously checking out the historical detail in this book, although I remain entirely responsible for any errors that may remain.

Gordon Edgar, Carlisle, April 2014.

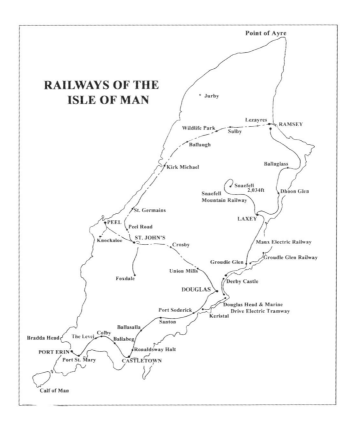

The journey begins at Douglas station, seen here on an early morning in September 1971. Little has changed to this day from this angle, apart from signage. The main station building is late Victorian and the adjacent office building, erected by 1888, is now home to the island's customs and revenue department, but was originally built as the railway's administrative offices, station bar, and directors' offices. In the peak of the railway's activity the main station building was home to the station masters' and porters' offices as well as storage space for many millions of card tickets and stored railway records. (Author's collection)

A classic early evening study of No. 4 *Loch* (Beyer Peacock works No. 1416, built in 1874) and No. 8 *Fenella* (Beyer Peacock W/No. 3610, built in 1894) at Douglas station, 9 April 2013.

The special train marking the reopening of the Castletown–Port Erin section of the system stands at Douglas station just after arrival from Port Erin on 2 June 1968, with No. 12 *Hutchinson* (Beyer Peacock W/No. 5126 of 1908). The Douglas–Port Erin line was the most profitable of all on the island and in the early 1950s there were nine daily weekday departures from Douglas and ten from Port Erin.

The platform side of the facade at Douglas station on a morning before the day's services commenced, believed to be in September 1971. (Author's collection)

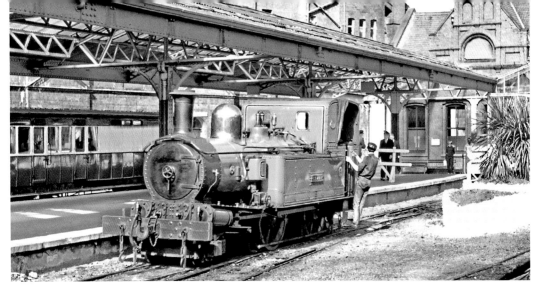

No. 10 *G. H. Wood* (Beyer Peacock W/No. 4662, built in 1905) runs round its train from Peel at Douglas station in the late 1960s. (Author's collection)

The official reopening special of the Port Erin line has just returned to Douglas station behind No. 12 *Hutchinson.* Dignitaries and guests in period costume stand in the station concourse area after the historic arrival on Sunday 2 June 1968.

It might be cold and windy, but how wonderful this experience was, seeing the small-boilered Beyer Peacock 2-4-0 tank No. 8 *Fenella* climbing the steeply graded line out of Douglas at Ellenbrook on such a clear morning, clearly demonstrating the infectious charm of this Manx railway.

For all looking like a St John's–Ramsey train of yesteryear, No. 8 *Fenella* looks delightful heading this short van and passenger rake high up on the headland at Keristal on 9 April 2013. Originating from 1894 and named after a character in a novel by Sir Walter Scott, popular at the time, this locomotive was for many years based on the Ramsey line of the railway and indeed remained in service through the Marquis of Ailsa revival in 1967. She carries a unique, 2-foot-10-inch-diameter, 160-psi boiler, which gives her the same theoretical power output as the medium boiler locomotives, but in reality she was inclined to run short of steam on heavy trains.

After climbing from Douglas to the summit at Keristal, the safety valves are lifting and the injectors are on as No. 12 *Hutchinson* drifts down the grade into Port Soderick station heading the 11.50 service train from Douglas to Port Erin on Tuesday 9 April 2013.

The 09.50 from Port Erin to Douglas with No. 4 *Loch* runs into Port Soderick as No. 8 *Fenella* waits for the single line token with a special charter train to Santon and Castletown on 8 April 2013.

Manx Northern Railway (MNR) 0-6-0 tank No. 4 *Caledonia* (Dubs & Co. W/No. 2178, built in 1885) rolls into Port Soderick heading the first train of the day from Douglas to Port Erin on 19 June 1999. The station building in the background is now privately owned. In the early 1950s Port Soderick was a request stop for all but the 16.20 ex-Port Erin service.

With a friendly wave from the young fireman to passengers sheltering from the rain under the Santon station canopy waiting for a Douglas train, No. 11 *Maitland* (Beyer Peacock W/No. 4663/1905) passes through the request stop heading an afternoon Douglas to Port Erin service on 19 June 1999. Santon (Yiarn Skylley Stondane) is the last on the line to still boast its original 1874 building, being of timber construction with corrugated iron roofing, painted in an orange and red style unchanged for many years. It includes the station master's accommodation and porter's rooms as well as a passenger waiting shelter recessed from the running lines. Until a major relaying of the entire railway in 2001 it was largely untouched for well over a century; this photograph was captured before those changes took place, which included the installation of platforms facing both tracks. The station's sheltered location boasts some magnificent exotic palm trees.

The fireman of No. 11 *Maitland* and guard of a morning Douglas–Port Erin service exchange conversation while waiting for the Douglas train to arrive on 24 April 1999. Ballasalla is the main passing point for service trains and the train from Douglas often arrives before the service from Port Erin. The 1985 brick-built station building on the raised Down side platform replaced a wooden structure originally erected on the Up side.

No. 11 *Maitland* stands at Ballasalla, waiting for a clear road, as No. 10 *G. H. Wood* approaches with a Port Erin–Douglas service on 24 April 1999. The crew from *Maitland* evidently had some exchange of information to make with the incoming crew of the locomotive from Port Erin.

The low afternoon sun just penetrates the splendid tunnel of trees west of the station as No. 8 *Fenella* gets underway from Castletown station on 8 April 2013. The former goods shed stands prominently and can be seen beyond the brake coach.

In the low afternoon sun and beneath the classic avenue of trees west of Castletown station, the former island's capital, No. 8 *Fenella* gets underway heading a service for Port Erin on 8 April 2013.

No. 4 *Caledonia* passes Poulsom Park on the western departure from Castletown on a wet 11 April 2013. The park, a large grassed area surrounded by iron railings, was provided and funded by a generous benefactor to the town and was established at around the same time as the railway. It is from this benefactor that the park takes its name.

No. 12 *Hutchinson* prepares to depart from Castletown on the 13.50 Douglas to Port Erin service as No. 8 *Fenella* stands in the adjacent platform heading a charter train on 8 April 2013.

With a flagged signal from the train guard, No. 4 *Caledonia* departs from Castletown heading a charter special for Port Erin on 10 April 2013. When the railway was first constructed, Castletown had until ten years previously been the island's capital and therefore a substantial station was provided there. The large cast concrete Triskelion or 'Legs of Mann', which appears set into a raised lawn area in front of the former goods shed at platform level, is believed to have originally been sited at the long-closed halt at Peel Road on the Ramsey Line, and was installed at Castletown in 1986.

Dubs 0-6-0 tank No. 4 *Caledonia* trundles through the delightful halt at Ballabeg with an afternoon Douglas to Port Erin service on 18 June 1999, which had no passengers to set down or pick up on this occasion.

Right: Ballabeg is a request stop for trains in both directions and here is a back-lit scene of its delightful 'station approach'. No. 11 *Maitland* steams through purposefully heading the first Douglas–Port Erin train of the day on 18 June 1999. The extant station building is used as a platelayer's hut, which has never been opened to provide passenger shelter. As a small concession to waiting passengers a veranda was added to the front of the station and a concrete platform area created in the winter of 1987. The site was further 'improved' in 2001 when a pumping station for the all-island sewer network was installed to the rear of the station and a platform to fit three coaches was added. This takes the form of a wall of sleepers which has been back-filled to provide a half-height platform for alighting and boarding passengers.

Below: No. 11 *Maitland* runs non-stop through Ballabeg Halt on 19 June 1999, heading a Douglas–Port Erin service. *Maitland* had the honour of hauling the Marquis of Ailsa's reopening train on 3 June 1967.

MNR No. 4 *Caledonia* passes through Colby station in the rain heading an afternoon charter from Castletown to Port Erin on 10 April 2013.

Colby Level Crossing halt and crossing keeper's hut on 20 June 1999; also referred to as 'The Level' (Yn Laare), this diminutive request stop serves the hamlets or individual houses of Level (Rushen), Croit-E-Caley, Kentraugh, Ballagawne and Ballakillowey. The 1-km section of line from the previous station (Colby) is straight and has a level crossing for Kentraugh Farm (seen in the distance). In February 2013 the crossing lodge and its environs were restored by volunteers from the Isle of Man Steam Railway Supporters' Association. Automatic barriers were introduced in 2002 and the manually operated gates were removed and since then the crossing keeper's hut has been unmanned, but it remains in situ housing storage facilities for the railway out of season. Also at that time a section of raised platform, of just one coach length, was installed at the request of a regular passenger.

Above: Port St Mary (Purt le Moirrey) station in the rain on 11 April 2013. As the April 2013 photographic charter organiser David Williams (in the flat cap) discusses a wet weather plan, some adventurous participants have had enough of the rain and, in anticipation of a tea break upon arrival at Port Erin station, promptly rejoin the train.

Right: 19 June 1999 was a day of persistent rain and Port St Mary has received its fair share yet again. The crossing keeper/ station master converses with the train crew as the train departs for Douglas. Automatic barriers have now been installed and the gatekeeper's tasks are no longer required. The former station master's dwelling can be seen opposite what was the makeshift station master's hut, located at the end of the platform.

Port Erin ticket hall on 10 April 2013. Following extensive refurbishment the station won an Ian Allan Heritage Railway award in 1990. The model is of *Mona's Queen*, built by Ailsa Shipbuilding in Troon. She was launched in December 1972, and her final voyage was 3 September 1990. The Whistle Stop Café is housed in the former porters' office, located off to the right of this photo.

Port Erin station area *c.* 1974, with No. 13 *Kissack* (Beyer Peacock W/No. 5382, built in 1910) moving from the shed and running onto its train. The Bus Vannin garage is seen under construction in what was the former bay platform and carriage stock storage area and was opened in 1975. (Author's collection)

Above: Douglas Corporation Transport fleet No. 64, registration No. KMN835, standing outside the 1975-built bus garage at Port Erin station yard on 10 April 2013. The vehicle is an AEC Regent III fitted with a Northern Counties H30/26R body from 1949.

Right: Probably in the mid-1970s, No. 13 *Kissack* blows off steam outside Port Erin shed alongside the original water tower, which was demolished in 1986. A one-off order from 1910 and named after company director E. T. Kissack, unlucky 13 (latterly referred to as 12a by some of the railway's staff) was one of the backbones of the railway's fleet, having seldom been out of service until withdrawn with a defective boiler at Christmas 1992. The boiler was refurbished and placed in the frames of No. 10 *G. H. Wood*, which re-entered service as part of the 'Year of Railways' in 1993, but No. 13 was left in dismantled form and stored. In 2001 it was announced that she would be the recipient of a new boiler and by the season of 2006 she was returned to steam. Painted in the contemporary fleet livery of 'Indian Red', her previous incarnation had been in a deep Brunswick green, not thought to have been an historic livery of the railway but more a preferred shade at the time. She carries the deeper whistle that she will be remembered for in the 1980s. No. 13 is a regular performer on the railway and part of the active fleet since returning to service in 2006 with a new boiler. (Author's collection)

Ex-County Donegal Railway (CDR) railcars built by Walker Bros of Wigan/GNR Dundalk Works (W/ Nos 79789/1949 and 83149/1950 respectively) stand in Douglas station forming the 14.05 departure to Castletown, on a very wet 31 May 1968. By the time of departure steady rainfall had set in, causing the railcar's wheels to slip furiously on the relentless 1 in 65 climb away from Douglas, providing an unforgettable and unique travel experience for the author. When purchased in 1961, the CDR running numbers 19 and 20 were retained by the IoMR – No. 20 is leading here. The cabs, along with the power bogies, were built by Walker Bros, but the passenger part of the railcar, which is articulated to the cab, was built at Dundalk Works.

In atrociously wet conditions on Friday 31 May 1968, the two ex-CDR railcars stand in the station, No. 19 nearest the camera. They then formed an unadvertised school special to Port Erin and back, on the yet to be officially reopened section of line. The author's Kodak Instamatic camera and transparency film were stretched beyond their limits in these grim conditions. The railcars were believed to have been purchased with the intention of deploying them on the Peel line. Due to no turntable being available at each end of the line they could not operate as single units, as they did in Ireland.

No. 11 *Maitland* runs round its carriages in the rain at Castletown, prior to returning to Douglas at 16.25. After reopening of the railways in 1967 by Lord Ailsa, 'Apple Green' was adopted as the standard fleet livery.

No. 11 *Maitland* gently simmers in the rain at Castletown before heading the 16.25 train back to the island's capital on Friday 31 May 1968. The lack of a raised platform was common at many stations on the island, hence the provision of the double row of footsteps on the coaches.

No. 8 *Fenella* brewing up on Douglas shed at lunchtime on Sunday 2 June 1968. There were no regular timetabled Sunday services on the railway during this era, but this day was special, as it was the official reopening of the Castletown–Port Erin extension. An enthusiast's special ran in the morning to Peel and return with Manx Northern Railway (MNR) No. 4 *Caledonia*, which was noted by the author departing from Douglas emitting steam from just about every gland possible. The afternoon special to Castletown and Port Erin, in which the author travelled, departed Douglas at 14.05 and was hauled by No. 12 *Hutchinson* with No. 8 *Fenella* banking on the rear to Port Soderick.

In 1968 the thrice-weekly Douglas–Ramsey service was double-headed from Douglas to St John's, where the train was split. The train locomotive for the Ramsey portion hauled locomotives out of the carriage shed for static display. No. 14 *Thornhill* (Beyer Peacock W/No. 2028/1880) in MNR red livery and No. 1 *Sutherland* (Beyer Peacock W/No. 1253/1873) are seen on display in the station yard on Monday 3 June 1968. Built for the MNR in 1880, at the same time as No. 7 *Tynwald*, this locomotive was originally allocated the fleet No. 3 by the MNR, only becoming No. 14 upon the merger with the Isle of Man Railway in 1905, but not receiving its number and chimney numeral immediately. Interestingly, it is recorded that *Thornhill* carried three name plates, one on each side of the tank as usual, and a third on the rear cab sheet. The destiny of this third plate remains a mystery to this day. She was the only locomotive purchased by the MNR to be built by Beyer Peacock & Co. and was similar in design to the smaller class locomotives of the Isle of Man Railway.

The locomotive was re-boilered no less than five times. Still being in the most 'original' form, she was unique in the fleet, retaining her distinctive Salter safety valves until withdrawal from service. After storage for several years she was one of the surplus locomotives to be repainted and placed on display at St John's during the 1967 and 1968 seasons, and later at Douglas station. Upon nationalisation in 1978 she was purchased for private preservation, together with MNR six-wheel coach 'N.45' and is currently not available for public viewing.

Another transparency where the Instamatic camera was seriously challenged. In heavily overcast conditions, No. 10 *G. H. Wood* runs round its train at Peel, having brought in the first service of the day, the 10.20 from Douglas on 31 May 1968. Despite services looking assured with a twenty-one-year lease agreed between the Marquis of Ailsa and the Isle of Man Railway, matters quickly went sour, and the last regular passenger service to Peel ran just over three months later, on 7 September 1968. Container carrying wagons, converted from passenger coaches, can be seen in the siding behind.

No. 10 *G. H. Wood* has just arrived at Ramsey on the thrice-weekly 10.20 service from Douglas, splitting at St John's, with an arrival at 11.37 on Monday 3 June 1968. The locomotive quickly detached from the stock to run round, and the author recalls that a brisk exit from the train was required in order to secure this shot in the head-shunt alongside the locomotive shed.

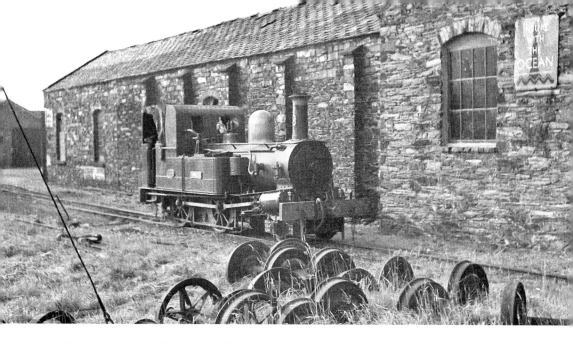

Regular performer on the Ramsey line, No. 8 *Fenella* runs alongside the locomotive shed at Ramsey *c.* 1960. The enamel advertising sign and abandoned wheelsets in the head-shunt area add much charm to the scene. (Author's collection)

After taking on water, No. 11 *Maitland* is seen setting back into Douglas station to take on a Port Erin service, believed to be in the early 1960s. (Author's collection)

Another possible late 1960s photo, as a father and his son pose alongside No. 11 *Maitland* at Douglas station, quite possibly taken by the mother of the family. Where is this young rail fan today? (Author's collection)

There is so much to feast the eye on in this photo taken from the end of Douglas station's platforms 5 and 6, looking towards the shed and yard. No. 11 *Maitland* is departing from the station. Outside the shed and workshop buildings are a pre-1959-registered Morris 1000 van, registration YMN494, and an early Mini, while inside is an ex-County Donegal railcar. The date is believed to be in the early 1960s. (Author's collection)

No. 12 *Hutchinson* makes a brisk start from Douglas at 16.25 with what possibly looks like the 16.20 to Peel in the summer 1967 season. No. 12 was a one-off order, similar in design to her two sisters purchased in 1905. Built in 1908 and named after company director W. A. Hutchinson, she was delivered to the railway with Salter safety valves and a deeper tone of whistle than had previously been employed. Still in service today, she has always been one of the most active members of the fleet, perhaps only surpassed by No. 11 *Maitland*. Of note is that she was one of only two engines (the other being No. 5) to carry a brass fleet number above the name plate on the tank. This was lost prior to the 1981 rebuild and was reinstated for the 2009 season. (Author's collection)

No. 10 *G. H. Wood* is the subject of conversation at Douglas station in the late 1960s. (Author's collection)

No. 4 *Loch* and No. 8 *Fenella* moving off shed at Douglas on 9 April 2013.

Activity such as this has been performed at Douglas shed for almost 140 years, apart from seasonal interruptions, and also in 1966 when it looked as though the railway in the Isle of Man would be closed for good, quite a sobering thought! Before the commencement of services on 9 April 2013, 0-6-0 tank No. 4 *Caledonia* moves off shed as 2-4-0 tank No. 8 *Fenella* is about to be lubricated prior to taking up her duties.

No. 10 *G. H. Wood* is moved into Douglas shed alongside No. 4 *Caledonia* on 11 April 2013.

Activity in the rain at Douglas shed on 11 April 2013, with ex-works No. 10 *G. H. Wood* in the green livery and No. 8 *Fenella* and No. 4 *Loch* moving into the shed after their day's duties.

Above: This image doesn't pretend to represent anything other than a 140-year-old steam locomotive shed still in everyday use, including strip lights, plastic tubing, warts and all. Preparing for the day's diagrams on Tuesday 9 April 2013, MNR No. 4 *Caledonia* and No. 8 *Fenella* move off from the atmospheric Douglas shed.

Right: Early morning activity around Douglas shed on 9 April 2013. No. 4 *Caledonia* shunts the stock forming a 'TT Press charter' as No. 4 *Loch* and No. 8 *Fenella* receive attention before their day's diagrams.

Above: No. 8 *Fenella* runs onto Douglas shed for coal and water before taking an evening charter train out to Keristal and Port Soderick. The trailing exhaust conceals the security fencing behind, alongside the bus depot, the site of the access to the railways former main goods and carriage sidings at Douglas.

Left: The first trains of the day on 8 April 2013 pass at Ballasalla. The 09.50 departure from Douglas to Port Erin, with No. 4 *Loch*, runs into Ballasalla as No. 12 *Hutchinson* waits for the token to proceed to Douglas.

Right: No. 10 *G. H. Wood* stands in the shed yard at Douglas as No. 4 *Caledonia* shunts a MNR van past the restored 1892 Dutton & Co. station signal box on 11 April 2013.

Below: Lubricants carried in the traditional Isle of Man Railway style, on the front of No. 8 *Fenella.*

MNR No. 4 *Caledonia* and Isle of Man Railways No. 8 *Fenella* stand alongside the station platform at Douglas (Doolish) on the evening of 9 April 2013.

No. 10 *G. H. Wood* resplendent in its fresh coat of 'Ailsa Green' paint standing in the rain outside Douglas shed on 11 April 2013, with Nos 8 *Fenella* and 4 *Loch* behind.

32

No. 8 *Fenella* climbs away from the capital and was captured at Ellenbrook on 8 April 2013.

On 9 April 2013 the 11.50 Douglas to Port Erin service works into Santon station, as a mother and two children wait to board the service. No. 8 *Fenella* stands in the adjacent platform at the head of a special charter train.

The Manx Northern Railway heraldic crest on the side of MNR Coach No. 17.

The fascinating illusion of perpetual mirrors and period photographs is seen in one of the Isle of Man Railway passenger coaches.

A historic Manx Northern Railway composition; No. 4 *Caledonia* on the climb at Ellenbrook with a MNR van and the unique 'Foxdale' coach.

An interior ceiling light in one of the Isle of Man Railway coaches. The author recalls during his visit in 1968 that some of these light glasses contained rain water that had leaked through the roof, with the water swirling about as the coach swayed from side to side on its journey!

Seen through the peacock-style window design in the former ladies' waiting room of the 1904-built station, the oldest working locomotive on the Isle of Man, No. 4 *Loch*, is stabled outside Port Erin shed shortly after arriving on the 15.50 from Douglas on Sunday 7 April 2013.

MNR No. 4 *Caledonia* framed in the main entrance to Castletown station on 11 April 2013. The station building was constructed in 1876 sourcing distinctive local grey limestone from nearby Scarlett Point.

MNR No. 4 *Caledonia* approaches Santon on 10 April 2013. *Caledonia*, originally purchased as a freight engine, was the only steam locomotive with the o-6-o wheel arrangement to work on the island, and had a tractive effort of 11,120 lb, making it the most powerful.

No. 12 *Hutchinson* seen through the station waiting room window, moving onto Port Erin shed for the night, having brought in the 15.50 departure from Douglas. The out-stationed locomotive would then take charge of the 09.50 departure to Douglas the following morning.

Left: The unusual sight of two locos moving onto Port Erin shed. Following disposal, No. 12 *Hutchinson* and No. 4 *Caledonia* move off the water column onto the shed during the late afternoon of 10 April 2013.

Below: MNR No. 4 *Caledonia* rests outside Port Erin shed on 10 April 2013.

Right: No. 12 *Hutchinson* reflected in a mirror in Port Erin shed on 10 April 2013.

Below: The cosy rest area at the rear of Port Erin shed on 10 April 2013. The guard of the charter train takes a well-earned rest after a full day, before a night photographic session begins, entailing further duties for him. There must have been a few interesting stories told around this fireplace over the years.

The familiar line of wheel sets outside the shed at Douglas sets the scene for No. 8 *Fenella*, seen departing in the 1950s. The neatly stacked coal stockpile, interlocked in dry stone wall fashion, is noteworthy, as is the systematic method of using the coal stockpile. (Author's collection)

No. 14 *Thornhill* seen at Douglas in the late 1950s. She was finally withdrawn with a weak boiler in 1963. (Author's collection)

An evocative late 1950s scene from the end of the platforms at Douglas station as an enthusiast makes those all-important notes for the sake of history. No. 8 *Fenella* receives final preparations for service and No. 16 *Mannin* (Beyer Peacock W/No. 6296, built in 1926) is coaled up by hand in the shed yard. The difference in the boiler sizes of these two Beyer Peacock locomotives, thirty-two years apart in construction, is prominent in this viewpoint. The William Priestman excavator outside the shed is also noteworthy. (Author's collection)

A general view of Douglas shed from the end of the station platforms in the late 1950s, with No. 5 *Mona* (Beyer Peacock W/No. 1417, built in 1874) simmering in the shed yard. In the 1950s there was always a flurry of activity at around 10.00 each morning with four engines coming off shed to take the 10.05 to Port Erin, 10.10 to Peel, 10.25 to Ramsey and another Port Erin service at 10.30. There was also the station pilot/banking locomotive to be seen lurking around. (Author's collection)

No. 13 *Kissack* makes a splendid sight storming away from Douglas in the late 1950s. The leading coach 'F12' was delivered from Brown Marshalls in 1881. (Author's collection)

A late 1950s scene as No. 8 *Fenella* has her boiler tubes cleaned as she stands in the carriage sidings, with loaded 'M' series two-plank open wagons ('M.73' being built by the Metropolitan Railway Carriage & Wagon Co. in 1925) and some 'K' series cattle wagons loaded with drums, possibly containing fish. The entire cattle wagon fleet had disappeared by 1975. (Author's collection)

The sheer bulk of No. 16 *Mannin* can be appreciated in this study of her at Douglas station in the 1950s, most probably on station pilot and banking duties. The last locomotive to be supplied to the railway and built in 1926, she was by far the most powerful 2-4-0T locomotive on the line. She was purchased to haul the heavy Port Erin boat train, a diagram which had previously taken two locomotives either double-headed or banked. Much larger than her older sisters, she was latterly used as a Peel-based engine and appears to have never travelled on the Ramsey line (certainly there is no photographic evidence to support this). She remained in service until 1964 and later was repainted into spring green and placed on static display at St John's and later Douglas stations, until entering the railway museum in 1975 with *Caledonia* and *Sutherland*. Never considered to be a candidate for restoration, she has only ventured out of the museum once (when it was being rebuilt in 1998/1999) and at this time she was treated to 'lining out' of paintwork, the previous coat having never been lined. This would possibly be the 'holy grail' of locomotive restoration projects on the island, as the locomotive is still in its original form; many would love to see this but it is unlikely to happen in the foreseeable future. (Author's collection)

No. 11 *Maitland* makes a spirited start from Douglas at precisely 10.00. This is believed to be a late 1950s photograph of possibly a Douglas–Castletown service. (Author's collection)

The water crane and locomotive preparation area at the end of No. 3 road, at Douglas station, with all manner of loco pieces and discarded items from this 1950s scene as No. 5 *Mona* departs from the station. (Author's collection)

A photograph believed to have been taken *c.* 1956. Schoolchildren board the afternoon train to Ballasalla and Douglas at Castletown hauled by No. 13 *Kissack*. The wooden station canopy originally had railings around the roof, but these had been removed by the time this photograph was taken. The entire canopy was removed during the winter 1993/94. (Author's collection)

No. 11 *Maitland* shuffles along past the rusty corrugated tin buildings of the Douglas carriage sheds, in the 1950s. The IoMR locomotives carried numbers on the rear of their cabs as an aid to identification when running cab first on all the return trips to Douglas. (Author's collection)

As the smoke from No. 12 *Hutchinson* drifts beneath the canopies, passengers hurry to embark on the 16.00 Castletown and Port Erin service at Douglas in the 1950s. (Author's collection)

The sheer bulk of No. 16 *Mannin* can be appreciated in this side-on study of her moving off Douglas shed in the 1950s. (Author's collection)

No. 5 *Mona* simmers between duties at the end of the Douglas station platforms on a summer's day in the 1950s. Arriving with No. 4 in 1874 in readiness for the opening of the Port Erin line, the name *Mona* was taken from the Latin for the Isle of Man. Rebuilt as a medium-boilered locomotive in 1911 and last re-boilered in 1946, No. 5 was a regular on the Peel line later in her career. She remained in service right up until the 1970 season, when she finally refused to hold a head of steam and was subsequently mothballed. After storage she was privately purchased from the newly nationalised railway in 1978 but remained on site, being stored in the 1893-built carriage shed at Douglas until it was demolished to make way for a new bus garage and administrative offices in 1998. She is currently in the back of the new carriage shed and has had no attention for many years, and is still wearing her 1967 spring green livery, now very faded. It is not known if she will ever return to service, but certainly in the near future this seems very unlikely. She was one of two (the other being No. 12) to carry a brass fleet numeral on the left-hand tank only. (Author's collection)

A fine study of an equally rather fine locomotive, No. 14 *Thornhill* stands at the coaling and watering point at Douglas in the 1950s. (Author's collection)

No. 14 *Thornhill* and No. 5 *Mona* prepare to depart from Douglas heading the morning service to Peel and Ramsey during the 1950s. (Author's collection)

A 1950s photo of No. 14 *Thornhill* and No. 5 *Mona* preparing to depart from Crosby heading the morning Douglas to Peel and Ramsey service, which will split at St John's. *Thornhill* was the only locomotive built for the MNR by Beyer Peacock in 1880. The line on the left served the cattle dock and goods shed. The station buildings were demolished and the site cleared in 1975, some seven years after the closure of the line, when the tracks were also lifted. (Author's collection)

A 1950s photograph showing No. 12 *Hutchinson* shunting and separating the stock for the Ramsey and Peel line services at St John's, having just backed past the signal box, and still with passengers on board. The incoming train would have had two locomotives on the front. The carriage shed is seen to the left of the signal box and the Foxdale line over the bridge behind the train. The twin signals behind the train show for Peel, the upper arm, and Ramsey, the lower arm. (Author's collection)

An interlude at St John's in the 1950s with the Peel train, headed by No. 5 *Mona*, waiting to depart, as the Ramsey train on the left, with No. 14 *Thornhill* in charge, stands in the platform. (Author's collection)

No. 14 *Thornhill* and No. 5 *Mona* heading Ramsey and Peel trains respectively at St Johns in the 1950s, as the Ramsey train guard looks on rather bemused at the photographer. (Author's collection)

A scene at Peel station in the 1950s, with an unidentified locomotive standing expectantly for passengers in the platform with coach 'F37'. (Author's collection)

A 1950s scene of Peel locomotive shed at the south end of the station, with No. 5 *Mona* simmering by the Mill Road level crossing waiting to take its return service to Douglas. A railway employee tends the small vegetable plot at the side of the shed, a perfect scene for the aspiring modeller. The station closed to passengers on 7 September 1968; however, a short-term goods service ran to Ramsey ran from Peel from 13 August 1968 until 29 April 1969. After this the station site became derelict and in 1973 the track on the Douglas to Peel line was sold for scrap and lifted. Today the station site is used as a car park and boat yard. The station building is still extant and many other features remain, but the locomotive shed was demolished at the same time as the rails were lifted, having become unsafe following a fire that engulfed the wooden lean-to some years previously, although the water tower beside it has survived and now forms part of a visitor's centre operated by the local heritage trust. This site also now houses one of the railway's original 1873 carriages which has been cosmetically restored in recent times. (Author's collection)

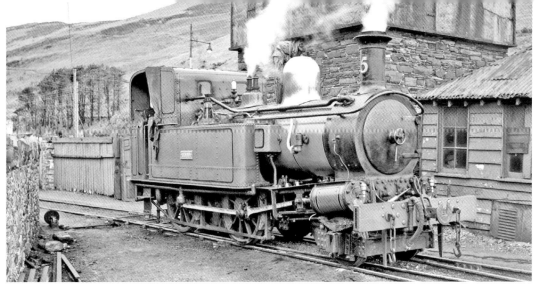

No. 5 *Mona* simmering alongside the water tower at Peel in the 1950s. The shed itself is located behind the tower, and beyond the shed are Peel Harbour and the River Neb. (Author's collection)

The 08.05 service to Douglas is just about to depart from Peel in the 1950s. The first two morning services from Peel to Douglas were taken over by buses from the winter 1959/60. No. 5 *Mona* is attached to a single coach, F37 (ex-MNR No. 16 built by Hurst Nelson in 1900), with the guard in conversation and the First Class compartment door open for the regular commuter arriving right on time from around the corner. His 35-minute journey time for the 12 miles to Douglas, swaying gently through the peaceful countryside in his compartment would enable a comfortable arrival time at his office, having set out at a very respectable time from his home in the small harbour town on the west coast of the island. The station, located next to the harbour, was opened on 1 July 1873. Service trains finally ceased on 7 September 1968 and the Manx Transport Museum Group have their headquarters in the nearby former brickworks office, holding a number of railway-related items. The terminus building seen here now forms a display area for the House of Mannanan, a museum dedicated to the island's history. (Author's collection)

No. 6 *Peveril* heading a Douglas–Peel service at St Johns in the 1950s. A one-off purchase in 1875 from Beyer Peacock & Co. (W/No. 1524), and of similar design to Nos 4 and 5, *Peveril* (named after a character in Sir Walter Scott's novel *Peveril of the Peak*) saw extensive use on the Peel line for many years, highly appropriate as the name is also of local origin. She was rebuilt as a 'medium-boilered' locomotive in 1911, and last re-boilered in 1932. She was withdrawn from service in August 1960, having been employed latterly as station shunter at Douglas, and stored out of use thereafter. In 1967, during the Marquess of Ailsa years, she was selected as one of the static display locomotives at St John's station and, after closure of the Peel and Ramsey lines in 1968, was relocated to Douglas Station for display purposes. Stored for several years together with No. 5 *Mona* in the original 1893 Douglas carriage shed, she was removed upon demolition and during 1994 was cosmetically restored by members of the Isle of Man Steam Railway Supporters' Association. She is now resident in the Port Erin railway museum and carries the 'Indian Red' livery of the post-war years. Sometimes considered as a restoration job by the railway, this has yet to be carried out, but enthusiasts remain hopeful that this may happen one day. (Author's collection)

Watched by a member of the St John's station staff, No. 12 *Hutchinson* makes a lively departure away from the station heading a Ramsey service in the 1950s. (Author's collection)

The guard is seen in conversation with the footplate crew of No. 14 *Thornhill* as they wait for departure time from St John's heading a Ramsey service under leaden skies in the 1950s. Two readable advertisements on the hoarding are extolling the virtues of beer being 'the best long drink in the world' and asserting that photographs 'come out best on Kodak film', two claims that would indeed be hard to disagree with! (Author's collection)

No. 8 *Fenella* heading a Ramsey service away from St John's in the 1950s. The lines to Ramsey (left) and Peel (right) ran parallel for a short distance and racing double departures were frequently witnessed, however the Ramsey driver had a short straw as the line was on a climbing gradient in the Ramsey direction. (Author's collection)

Being keenly observed by an enthusiast who has travelled on the incoming service from Douglas, No. 14 *Thornhill* runs round its carriages immediately after arrival at Ramsey. In the early 1950s seven trains left Ramsey each weekday, with eight making the 25-mile journey from Douglas. Industrial units now occupy the Ramsey station site. (Author's collection)

The 3-foot-gauge, four-wheel petrol mechanical Wickham railcar (W/No. 5763, built in 1950) at the seaward end of the Queen's Pier at Ramsey in the 1950s. The Queens Pier has the distinction of being only the second pier to have been erected on the island and is now the only one to have survived. Commissioned by the Isle of Man Harbour Board and constructed by the well-known firm of Head Wrightson & Company, this 2,241-foot (679-m) pier was opened on 22 July 1886 by the Lord Bishop of Sodor and Man. Built at a cost of £45,000 Ramsey Queens Pier was designed purely as a landing point for steamers plying the Liverpool, Fleetwood, Belfast and River Clyde routes. Because of this Ramsey Queens Pier has never seen the development of leisure facilities, similar to those found at many other piers around our coastline. It comprised a wooden deck over iron piles, and had a small café at the seaward end. (Author's collection)

The Isle of Man Harbour Commissioners' 3-foot gauge Wickham railcar and the original locomotive, Frank Hibberd 'Planet' four-wheel petrol mechanical (W/No. 2027, built in 1937), stand at the landward end of the pier in June 1957. The 3-foot-gauge horse-drawn tramway that was originally used to transport building materials during construction ran down the centre of the deck and was retained for baggage transport. The horse-drawn tramway was finally motorised in 1937 when the 8-hp petrol 'Planet' locomotive was introduced, but little else of note occurred until after the Second World War. Modifications were again made to the tramway in 1950 when this Wickham railcar was added, followed by some track alterations in 1956, giving the line an overall length of 2,080 feet (631m). The railcar can now be found on the IoMR and the Hibberd locomotive can be found at Jurby Transport Museum. (Author's collection)

A late 1950s view of the Queen's Pier at Ramsey with the Wickham railcar at the seaward end. The first pier was built at Douglas in 1869 but was sold and re-erected at Rhos-on-Sea, North Wales, in 1896. The Queen's pier is now sadly closed and substantial investment will be required to restore it to public access again. (Author's collection)

Manx Electric Railway (MER) No. 22, the fourth and final 'Winter Saloon' delivered to the railway in 1899 and built by G. F. Milnes, in the short-lived 'Nationalisation' green-and-white livery awaiting departure from Ramsey for Derby Castle in the late 1950s. Running as a single car without a 'toast-rack' trailer would suggest this photo to have been taken out of the peak season. No. 22 was one of three 'Winter Saloon's repainted into this unpopular 'austerity' livery in 1958, but reverted back to its traditional appearance by 1960. (Author's collection)

MER 'Winter Saloon' No. 22 in the late 1950s 'austerity' livery rolls into Ballaglass Glen, approximately 5 miles away from Ramsey. The stop serves the nearby glen of the same name. The rustic wooden waiting shelter was demolished in 1985 and replaced with one fitted with a gate, allegedly to stop sheep getting trapped inside. (Author's collection)

MER forty-eight-seat 'Winter Saloon' No. 21 at Ramsey on 25 April 1999. No. 21 was supplied by G. F. Milnes of Birkenhead in 1899. To maintain the frequent service throughout the year the fleet consisted of twenty-four motor cars and twenty-four trailers.

MER 'Winter Saloon' No. 20 and Snaefell Mountain Railway (SMR) No. 6 stand at Laxey in the late 1950s. MER No. 20 was one of the cars selected for a repaint in 1957 upon nationalisation, carrying the experimental but unpopular 'austerity' green-and-white livery for a short time. (Author's collection)

MER Winter Salon No. 21 and a 'toast-rack' coach at Ramsey terminus on Saturday 1 June 1968.

SMR car No. 5 at Laxey station on 1 June 1968. Laxey is the main interchange station between the 3-foot-gauge MER and the 3-foot-6-inch-gauge SMR.

SMR car No. 6 at Bungalow station level crossing in the late 1950s. The road is the main A18 mountain road which forms part of the TT racing circuit, the annual event apparently imminent judging by the roadside banners already in place. Snaefell summit at just over 2,000 feet above sea level looms behind. (Author's collection)

MER 'Vestibuled Saloon' No. 7 at Laxey on a Ramsey–Douglas service on 1 June 1968.

SMR car No. 6 at the summit in the late 1950s. The railway climbs 1,820 feet during the almost 5-mile run from Laxey, with a ruling gradient of 1 in 12. On a clear day it is possible to see parts of England, Scotland, Ireland and Wales from the 2,034-foot summit of Snaefell. (Author's collection)

The Nationalised SMR began on the 1 June 1957, with a new livery for the cars being introduced over the winter of 1958/59. This green-and-white 'austerity' livery was only applied to cars No. 2 and No. 4, which after much complaint disappeared by 1963. Cars No. 2 and 3 stand outside the SMR shed at Laxey. (Author's collection)

MER 'Winter Saloon' No. 21 stands at Laxey with the SMR overhead line inspection tower wagon alongside on 25 April 1999.

SMR car No. 3 stabled at Laxey in the late 1950s. (Author's collection)

MER 'Winter Saloon' No. 22 in the green-and-cream livery at Laxey in the late 1950s. The Isle of Man Government control of the electric railway came into effect in 1957. (Author's collection)

MER 'Winter Saloon' No. 22 arrives at Laxey from Ramsey on 25 April 1999. It has just passed the Mines Tavern, a popular island watering hole and owned by the railway prior to 1957.

MER car No. 5, photographed at Laxey in the late 1950s, was the second of six 'Tunnel Cars' (named such after their long and sleek interiors) ordered for the Laxey extension of the MER in 1894. The car was built by G. F. Milnes and delivered with Milnes Series 3 trucks, fitted with Mather & Platt electrical gear along with longitudinal seats with a capacity for thirty-six passengers. In 1903 many cars were refurbished with new equipment, and car No. 5, in line with four other 'Tunnel Cars', gained Brush 'D' trucks and air brake equipment. In 1969 its original twin-piece cab windows were replaced with a sole central window. The vehicle remains in service today, after an overhaul and repaint in 2012. (Author's collection)

MER 'Winter Saloon' No. 20 at Derby Castle, Douglas, on 7 April 2013.

MER car No. 22 (in the Nationalised livery) at the Derby Castle terminus and Douglas Horse Tram No. 22 in the shed at Derby Castle in the late 1950s. The rustic booking office, built in 1898, is now the sole remaining Isle of Man Tramway and Electric Power Co. structure at the terminus. (Author's collection)

MER car No. 6, seen at Derby Castle on 7 April 2013, was built by G. F. Milnes of Birkenhead and delivered to the island with its five classmates in 1894. No. 6 underwent a full repaint during November 2010 at Derby Castle works into the MER red/white/teak livery.

Above: MER 'Winter Saloon'
No. 20 in Nationalisation
livery of the late 1950s
and 'toast-rack' open No.
46 at Laxey in June 1958.
(Author's collection)

Right: MER 'Winter Saloon'
No. 20 runs round 'toast-
rack' trailer No. 41 at Derby
Castle, Douglas, on 7 April
2013. No. 20 returned to
traffic during May 2010
after repairs and various
storage periods in 2008
and 2009. It is now in
regular service and forms
the mainstay of the MER
fleet alongside the other
three 'Winter Saloons'.

A Douglas Corporation Horse Tram with car No. 18 on the Promenade near the MER Derby Castle terminus on 1 June 1968. The Morris 1000 car and poster on the tramcar advertising Tommy Steele's 'Half a Sixpence' production dates the image. 140 years of operation of the Tramway will be celebrated in 2016, the tram services being inaugurated by Thomas Lightfoot in 1876.

A 1950s view of the Derby Castle interchange between the Douglas Horse Tram and the Manx Electric Railway. The flat fare on the Horse Tram was 6d, while return tickets on the MER were Laxey 3/6d, Ramsey 5/- and a two-day Rover Ticket was 10/-. (Author's collection)

The horse tram depot clock shows 09.39 on a pleasant late 1950s morning at the Derby Castle terminus, interchange for the Manx Electric Railway. Horse Tram 43 is in use with car 47 visible inside the shed. (Author's collection)

A late 1950s photo of the Douglas Horse Tramway on the Promenade with forty-seater car No. 43, built by the United Electric Car Co. Ltd in 1907. Ken Mackintosh was billed at the Villa Marina, as advertised on the side of the car. (Author's collection)

Douglas Corporation Horse Tram No. 43 and Douglas Corporation bus No. 55 (registration No. GMN906, an AEC Regent III built in 1947) at the Grand Hotel, Douglas, in the 1950s. This has now been the last surviving horse tramway in the British Isles for over half a century. (Author's collection)

A Douglas Corporation-owned horse stands patiently with its tram car No. 43 near the Queen Victoria Pier, Douglas, in the 1950s. The 3-foot-gauge tramway operates on a 1.6-mile stretch along the Douglas Promenade from Derby Castle at the north end to the Sea Terminal at the south end. (Author's collection)

Change round of the horse near the Queen Victoria Pier, Douglas, during a 1950s evening. The horses are very well cared for and during the winter months graze in fields around the island specially reserved for them. During the operating season they are stabled near the Derby Castle terminus and only work four return trips each in any one day. (Author's collection)

The Isle of Man Railway had its own delivery vans and here is No. 6 in their fleet, registration 8661MN, in the Douglas station concourse outside the booking office, probably during the 1960s. (Author's collection)

A delightful posed image of the driver of No. 11 *Maitland* chatting to a young admirer on the platform. It is a sunny summer's day *c.* 1967 and the station booking hall clocks show that it is 16.00. (Author's collection)

No. 4 *Loch* shunting the works train in the siding alongside Douglas station on 7 April 2013.

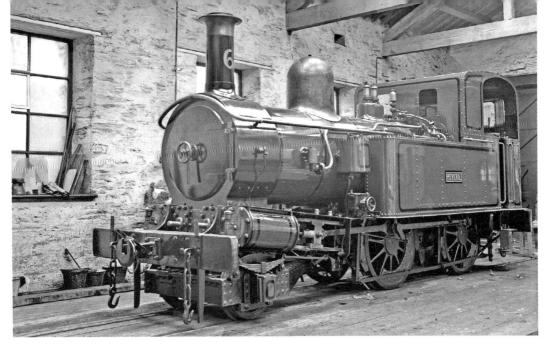

A photograph of No. 6 *Peveril* taken sometime between 1932 and 1938 inside the works at Douglas, bearing the unlined 'Indian Red' livery and apparently in ex-works condition. This loco is now housed in the Port Erin Museum alongside the station in the former bus garage. (Author's collection)

The horizontal steam engine at the rear of Douglas workshops, supplied in the late nineteenth century by John Chadwick & Son, Prince's Bridge Iron Works, Prince's Bridge, Water Street, Manchester. Although it is in full working order, it is now used just for demonstration purposes.

Motor Rail 'Simplex' four-wheel diesel mechanical (W/No. 40S280, built in 1966) in Douglas works. The yellow 'Simplex' was built for use at National Coal Board Kilnhurst Colliery in Yorkshire. It arrived on the island in October 1996, and has been used on both the IoMR and the MER. It has been used for shunting at Laxey Car Shed, although it is not known to have worked any passenger workings while on the MER.

The white loco, No. 18, a four-wheel diesel hydraulic, is named *Ailsa* and was built in 1990 by Hunslet-Barclay Ltd at Kilmarnock (Hunslet-Barclay W/No. 770 and Hunslet W/No. 9446). It was subsequently rebuilt by Hunslet in 1995 (W/No. 9342) and was used by the contractors who re-laid the Santon–Port Erin section of the line in conjunction with the IRIS all-island sewage project. It was originally built to 3-foot-gauge for use on Channel Tunnel works trains, but was subsequently re-gauged to 2-feet and used in conjunction with the Jubilee Line extension of the London Underground, then re-gauged again for use on the island. It has a restricting maximum speed of 8 mph, so is only unsuitable for shunting duties and use on the weed-killing train. It was bought from the contractors upon completion of the contract work and named *Ailsa* in honour of the man who did so much to keep the railway alive in the late 1960s.

Former Groudle Glen Railway 2-foot-gauge Bagnall 2-4-0 tank *Polar Bear* (W/No. 1781, built in 1905), sister loco to *Sea Lion*, receives some care at the Amberley Museum near Arundel on 6 July 2009. The locomotive has been returned to its original 'Fair Ground' livery which it carried when on the Isle of Man. Polar Bear left the island in 1967, going to the Brockham Museum near Dorking in Surrey, and during the period 1968–1971 the author, as a volunteer, assisted with its part-restoration before the museum closed and the stock transferred to Amberley Museum in West Sussex.

Above: The inhospitably wet conditions of 20 June 1999 ensured that there were no takers for the picnic bench at Sea Lion Rocks station on the Groudle Glen Railway. *Sea Lion*, a 2-4-0 tank built by W. G. Bagnall of Stafford (W/No. 1484, built in 1896) stands at the end of the line on the headland overlooking the Irish Sea towards mainland England. The 2-foot-gauge line was opened in 1896, when the Glen was developed as a tourist attraction and zoo and apart from closure during the two world wars, operated until the end of the 1962. The stock was sold and dispersed and it wasn't until May 1986 that the railway was officially reopened, with the original Sea Lion Rocks terminus on the headland being subsequently reopened in 1992.

Right: The Douglas Head Marine Drive Tramway was opened in 1896 by the New General Traction Company and operated until 1939. It took passengers from Douglas Head (reached by Ferry and Incline Railway) to Port Soderick (where a cliff lift could be used to reach the beach below). It never reopened after the war, and was largely lifted and destroyed by 1955. After closure the rolling stock remained in the depot until

1951–52 before being scrapped, except for one motor car which was retrieved for preservation at the National Tramway Museum at Crich in Derbyshire, where it resides to this day. This line was unique on the island by using conventional standard-gauge, double-deck trams with toast-rack seating downstairs, the fleet comprising a total of sixteen open-top vehicles, eight motor cars and eight trailers. A survivor of the system, seen in this early 1950s photograph with Douglas Bay beyond, is the derelict Walberry Viaduct and the cast-iron poles for the overhead wiring still extant. The Marine Drive roadway was reinstated in 1956 after some seven years of work, but the roadway has been closed for several years owing to a number of serious landslides. The route of this unique lost railway provides a spectacular view of the Irish Sea, and forms part of the Isle of Man's coastal footpath Raad ny Foillan (Way of the Gull), created in 1986. (Author's collection)

In 1886 the Foxdale Railway Company opened a 2.5-mile-long branch from St Johns to Foxdale for the purpose of serving mineral extraction. The line was operated by an agreement with the Manx Northern Railway. The brick station building was constructed in 1886, although the branch was intended primarily for freight traffic. Taken over by the Isle of Man Railway in 1905, passenger trains continued to run to Foxdale until 1943 when the service was withdrawn, although the station saw little passenger use, as from 1940 many services had been substituted by a bus. Goods services continued on the branch until 1960. It was not lifted though until the mid-1970s. This is a 1950s photograph with all track work and the ground frame in situ. (Author's collection)

No. 12 *Hutchinson* augments the stock in the Douglas station platform on Sunday 2 June 1968, for the afternoon reopening special to Port Erin. The coach being added, 'F25', was originally built in 1896 as a bogie vehicle.

No. 8 *Fenella* shunts stock past Douglas signal box on 9 April 2013.

On 10 April 2013, No. 4 *Loch* drifts down the grade into Port Soderick, passing the signal windlass controlling the approach signal, but locked out of use.

The present-day late Victorian Douglas station buildings in red Ruabon brick and seen behind the locomotives were constructed between 1887 and 1913, replacing timber constructions established upon the opening of the line in 1873. After 1909 the station site was not significantly altered until 1978/79, when it was reduced to about half of its maximum size and the canopies were removed. The office block behind and dwarfing the station buildings was constructed in 1988. In its heyday, Douglas station sprawled across the sites of the present station, and the Bus Vannin garage and offices. The south side of station site has undergone much redevelopment in recent years. Much of the former freight yard is now occupied by a Tesco supermarket and the site of carriage shed and yard by the bus depot. The station is now consigned to the north side of the site reduced to one island platform with dedicated run round loops and one siding on the far north of the station, added during modifications in 1999 to create further outdoor storage for non-passenger vehicles. The vehicular entrance to the station yard is also the bus stop for connecting services between the railway and the island's bus services. The oldest working locomotive on the railway, No. 4 *Loch*, built in 1874, stands proudly at the shed entrance, with small-boilered No. 8 *Fenella* standing in one of the station platforms.

Left: No. 4 *Caledonia* framed in the A5 Douglas–Port Erin road overbridge as it departs from Santon heading a charter for Castletown on 10 April 2013.

A bridge that justifies a photograph despite the adjoining tree growth and the installation of safety rails is that which crosses the Silver Burn at Castletown. The small river rises near the South Barrule, flows under the Monk's Bridge at Ballasalla, reaching the sea at Castletown harbour. The Isle of Man Steam Railway crosses the river over this splendid stone bridge just on the west side of the station. On 9 April No. 4 *Loch* drifts across the bridge heading the 15.50 Port Erin–Douglas service train.

No. 4 *Loch* crosses the River Dhoo alongside the Douglas Nunnery, climbing the 1 in 65 grade on the outskirts of Douglas, the 09.50 to Port Erin on Sunday 7 April 2013. Trees and vegetation increasingly encroaching the lineside and river at Nunnery Woods have unfortunately made a clear viewpoint of the girder bridge virtually impossible, and even this composition is only just available while the tree branches are bereft of leaves.

No. 8 *Fenella* passes under the main Douglas–Port Erin road bridge at Santon on 8 April 2013.

In soft early evening sunlight, No. 8 *Fenella* passes the now out of use home signal alongside flooded fields on the approach to Port St. Mary station on 8 April 2013.

At the end of the 1 in 65 climb from Douglas and before the descent into Port Soderick, 3-foot-gauge 1894-built Beyer Peacock 2-4-0 tank No. 8 *Fenella* is captured high above the Irish Sea at Keristal during a David Williams photographic charter on the Isle of Man Steam Railway on 9 April 2013.

The clouds are rolling in from the west signalling a dramatic change in the weather compared to the previous weeks of snow and bitterly cold easterly winds. The daffodils on the bank are just starting to blossom, but at least the lower level of water flowing down the burn enabled a wider viewpoint to be had for No. 8 *Fenella* heading the MNR van and two coaches away from Santon on Tuesday 9 April 2013.

Having just surmounted the climb at 1 in 65 to the summit, No. 8 *Fenella* trundles down towards Port Soderick at Keristal, just before sunset on 9 April 2013.

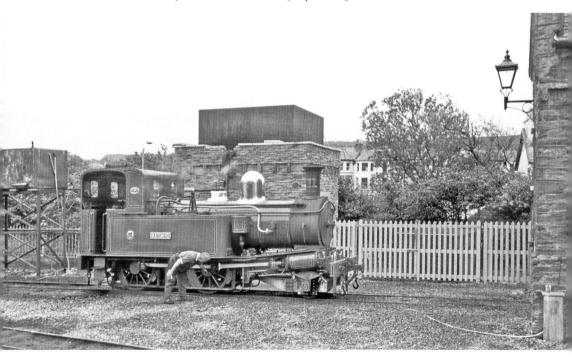

No. 11 *Maitland* receives attention at Port Erin shed prior to returning with a service to Douglas on 19 June 1999.

On 9 April 2013, No. 8 *Fenella* is prepared at Douglas shed for its day's duties.

The fireman of No. 8 *Fenella* tops up the water at Ballasalla, getting a shower in the process, while waiting for the single line section staff to proceed on to Castletown on 8 April 2013.

Above: No. 11 *Maitland* taking on water at Douglas in the early 1960s, the overflowing tank on the left showing that the task has just about been completed. The laborious but necessary job of ash disposal is being carried out in the background. (Author's collection)

Left: Three local lads, in time-honoured tradition, excitedly wait at the level crossing gate as No. 8 *Fenella* runs past. The 1894-built Beyer Peacock was running around the passenger coaching stock at Port Erin and would draw it out of the station's single platform for overnight storage. This image was not set up in any way and the young boys ran from the adjacent Athol Park to the crossing gates when the locomotive appeared, and rather cheekily sat on or peered through the gates in front of the photographer. The station is unique in having a public right of way bisecting the long platform and, in bygone days, longer trains (rarely seen today) would have to uncouple while loading prior to departure, to ensure the right of way to the nearby park was not blocked.

Manx resident and rail fan Ian Quiggin watches in the rain as No. 4 *Caledonia* positions its coaching stock at Colby station as part of a photographic charter on 11 April 2013. The loop at Colby station does not generally see much use, only when an additional service such as this charter is in the southern section and a service train is imminent.

Colby Level Crossing gates and the crossing keeper's hut on 20 June 1999. Automatic barriers were introduced in 2002 and the manually operated gates were removed. Until recently the road that leads to the level crossing also served the local Level Garage, and until well into the 1990s trains carried motor parts from Douglas for dropping off at this point; the garage was closed in 2000 and the site has since been redeveloped into residential housing. The village that has built up around the level crossing site has been expanded considerably since the arrival of the railway, happily making the halt frequently utilised during the summer months.

No. 12 *Hutchinson* crossing the A5 road at Ballasalla level crossing, *c.* July 1964 with a morning Douglas–Port Erin service, seen through the windscreen of a period delivery van. (Author's collection)

No. 8 *Fenella* seen through the driver's window of a 1931 Swift 10 HP 'Crusader' fabric sun saloon at Santon on 8 April 2013.

A Sentinel class 'S4' steam wagon (W/No. 8980, built in 1934) at Santon, as No. 8 *Fenella* heads a charter train alongside. In 1934 Sentinel launched a new and advanced steam wagon, the 'S type' which had a single-acting, four-cylinder, under-floor engine with longitudinal crankshaft and an overhead worm-drive axle. Their Sentinel Waggon Works design of the 1930s led to the production of 3,750 Sentinel 'Standards', the biggest selling steam lorry ever. It was lighter than previous designs and featured a modernised driver's cab with a set-back boiler and was available in four-, six- and eight-wheel form, designated S4, S6 and S8. In spite of its sophisticated design, however, it could not compete with contemporary diesel trucks for all-round convenience and payload capacity, and was phased out in the late 1930s.

A Foden flatbed truck bearing the R. G. Corlett's Laxey Flour Mills company colours and No. 4 *Caledonia* at Santon on 10 April 2013.

An exchange of flour from road to rail being re-enacted at Castletown station goods yard on 10th April 2013. Castletown station has always been one of the most active on the line, providing a source of much freight and goods traffic over the years. The town itself was considered to be second only to Douglas in importance to the island; with its bustling harbour and active agricultural scene, the station's importance remained until the final days of operation with livestock being transported from the station's cattle dock (the remains of which are on the right) until the final year the railway operated its full network.

No. 11 *Maitland* gets away from Santon heading a Douglas to Port Erin morning train on 20 June 1999, as a school party waits to board the Douglas train, which will cross with this one at Ballasalla, the next station down the line.

Taking a break from shunting cattle trucks in the siding at Castletown station, the driver of 1894-built Beyer Peacock 2-4-0 tank, No. 8 *Fenella*, chats with the owner of a 1931 Swift 10 HP 'Crusader' fabric sun saloon. A timeless scene recreated on 8 April 2013.

Recreating an Isle of Man freight transfer scene of yesteryear, a box van is shunted into the siding at Castletown, while a flatbed truck waits for its goods. Goods traffic was at one time an important feature of the IoMR, which was responsible for transporting regular consignments of milk, vegetables and livestock, as well as bulk materials such as coal, timber and ballast.

No. 4 *Loch* on the 1 in 65 climb away from Douglas at Ellenbrook on 9 April 2013.

No. 8 *Fenella* heads a traditional rake befitting of this smaller locomotive. In tow is ex-MNR 'G' class ventilated van No. 15 (originally used for livestock) built by the Swansea Wagon Company in 1879, heavily rebuilt coach 'F54', and coach 'F49' built as a bogie vehicle by MRCW in 1926. *Fenella* is the sole representative of the smaller engines and was generally employed on lighter trains, especially on the Ramsey line, as well as specials and station pilot duties at Douglas. *Fenella* is distinctive for her smaller appearance, giving a more graceful look than the more workhorse-like larger locomotives.

Right: The owner of a 1931 Swift 10 hp 'Crusader' fabric sun saloon watches the arrival of Isle of Man Railway 1894-built No. 8 *Fenella* at Santon station on 8 April 2013.

Below: The Isle of Man Steam Railway Beyer Peacock 2-4-0 tanks are feisty locomotives and well capable of handling the heaviest of trains on the island comprising up to six or seven loaded coaches. The eighth locomotive to arrive for the IoMR, *Fenella* was delivered in 1894. She ran in service right up until withdrawal after the 1968 season and is seen here at speed on the 1 in 65 climb out of Douglas near Ellenbrook on 8 April 2013.

No. 8 *Fenella* heads across the headland at Keristal shortly before sunset on 9 April 2013.

Typifying the rural charm of the Isle of Man Railway that the author first experienced on his visit in 1968, No. 8 *Fenella* emerges into the bright sunlight from Crogga Woods, on the final assault of the 1 in 112 grade to the summit of the line between Douglas and Port Erin, approximately 4 miles out of Douglas.

Built in 1878, the 'fairytale castle' of Crogga dominates the coastal skyline of the Isle of Man and is known by the local people as Crogga Castle. It is one of the most admired properties on the island and is home to the private 7.25-inch gauge Crogga Valley Railway. No. 8 *Fenella* passes Crogga during a photographic charter on 9 April 2013. All photographs taken on the private land of the Crogga Estate were obtained with the kind permission of the owners during the 2013 photographic charter organised by David Williams.

No. 8 *Fenella* climbs through Crogga Woods towards the line's summit, passing a recently cleared area of the Crogga Estate on 8 April 2013.

No. 8 *Fenella* rounds the curve over Crogga Glen on the 1 in 142 climb through the private Crogga Castle estate.

A clear view of the reverse curve just below Crogga Castle has been opened up with the recent tree felling, and No. 8 *Fenella* is seen with the MNR van and two coaches heading for Santon on 9 April 2013.

Nearing the end of the climb to the highest point on the Douglas–Port Erin line, No. 8 *Fenella* rounds the curve at Crogga Glen on 8 April 2013.

With ivy and brambles providing the only sign of greenery during this very late Spring of 2013, a late winter's scene is conveyed in this image of No. 12 *Hutchinson* in the woods above Port Soderick Glen, heading the 11.50 Douglas to Port Erin service train on Monday 8 April 2013.

MNR No. 4 *Caledonia* stands at Port Erin station, with an AEC Regent bus at the adjacent Bus Vannin garage.

Following completion of its two round trips on Douglas–Port Erin service trains, No. 4 *Loch* has its fire thrown out by the young fireman. Douglas shed yard is overlooked by the signal box, the last surviving on the railway. Built in 1892 and located at the end of the yard, the thirty-six-lever frame signal box was built by Dutton & Co. of Worcester and supplied to the railway when the yard was further modified and at the same time as the workshops were extended. The box remained in use until the summer of 1970 when the linkage was replaced with hand operated point levers in the yard. Since that time the building has been relocated to make way for the new transport headquarters and Bus Vannin garages. It was moved forward in 1998 from its original site at the same time as the 1893 carriage shed was demolished, and it remains out of use to this day.

With Milners Tower standing prominently on the Bradda Head headland, the final train of the day from Douglas drifts down the grade into Port Erin, journey's end, on 7 April 2013. The leisurely and enchanting journey of almost 16 miles will have taken one hour and five minutes. On a clear day the renowned Port Erin sunset across the sea can be enjoyed.

Obtaining a satisfactory sunset image on the Isle of Man Steam Railway is not as straightforward as it might appear, despite the twists and turns of the line, heading roughly north-east to south-west from Douglas to Port Erin. Even the crew of charter trains have a home to go to, and the locomotive requires watering and disposal. This was captured on the final run of the day at Keristal from the east side, but the sun had still not dipped quite low enough. Small-boilered No. 8 *Fenella* breasts the summit at Keristal before the descent into Port Soderick, prior to running around and returning to Douglas.

Vickers Viscount 701, registration number G-AMOA, was photographed at the airport on 3 June 1968, being prepared for the author's return flight to Manchester after four magical days on the island. The aircraft was subsequently damaged beyond repair in a heavy landing at Lulsgate Airport, Bristol, on 19 January 1970. The British-built Vickers Viscount was the first turbo-prop airliner in the world. It saw service with many airliners and freight operators throughout the world. The oldest surviving Viscount, G-ALWF, is now preserved at the Imperial War Museum Duxford, Cambridgeshire. Cambrian Airways was a Welsh airline based in Cardiff and started operations in 1935. It was subsequently incorporated into British Airways when BOAC, BEA, Cambrian and Northeast merged on 1 April 1974.

Any trip to the island starts and finishes by either ferry or plane. It is always a sad time to bid farewell to the island and this 1950s scene from a ferry sailing away from Douglas harbour shows the time of that deflating moment upon leaving the island, an experience that many readers of this book will have had – au revoir! (Author's collection)